ON CHRISTIAN HOPE

SPE SALVI

ENCYCLICAL LETTER

BENEDICT XVI

ENCYCLICAL LETTER

SPE SALVI
OF THE SUPREME PONTIFF
BENEDICT XVI
TO THE BISHOPS
PRIESTS AND DEACONS
MEN AND WOMEN RELIGIOUS
AND ALL THE LAY FAITHFUL
ON CHRISTIAN HOPE

Publication No. 7-039

United States Conference of Catholic Bishops

Washington, D.C.
ISBN 978-1-60137-039-6

Published in the United States, December 2007

CONTENTS

ON CHRISTIAN HOPE

Introduction

1. *"Spe salvi facti sumus"*—in hope we were saved, says Saint Paul to the Romans, and likewise to us (*Rom* 8:24). According to the Christian faith, "redemption"—salvation—is not simply a given. Redemption is offered to us in the sense that we have been given hope, trustworthy hope, by virtue of which we can face our present: the present, even if it is arduous, can be lived and accepted if it leads towards a goal, if we can be sure of this goal, and if this goal is great enough to justify the effort of the journey. Now the question immediately arises: what sort of hope could ever justify the statement that, on the basis of that hope and simply because it exists, we are redeemed? And what sort of certainty is involved here?

Faith is hope

2. Before turning our attention to these timely questions, we must listen a little more closely to the Bible's testimony on hope. "Hope," in fact, is a key word in Biblical faith—so much so that in several passages the words "faith" and "hope" seem interchangeable. Thus the *Letter to the Hebrews* closely links the "fullness of faith" (10:22) to "the confession of our hope without wavering" (10:23). Likewise, when the *First Letter of Peter* exhorts Christians to be always ready to give an answer concerning the *logos*—the meaning and the reason—of their hope (cf. 3:15), "hope" is equivalent to "faith." We see how decisively the self-understanding of the early Christians was shaped by their having received the gift of a trustworthy hope, when we compare the Christian life with life prior to faith, or with the situation of the followers of other religions. Paul reminds the Ephesians that before their encounter with Christ they were "without hope and without God in the world" (*Eph* 2:12). Of course he knew they had had gods, he knew they had had a religion, but their gods had proved questionable, and no hope emerged from their contradictory myths. Notwithstanding their gods, they were "without God" and consequently found themselves in a dark world, facing a dark future. *In nihil ab nihilo quam cito recedimus* (How quickly we fall back from nothing to nothing):[1] so says an epitaph of that period. In this phrase we see in no uncertain terms the point Paul was making. In the same vein he says to the Thessalonians: you must not "grieve as others do who have no hope" (*1 Th* 4:13). Here too we see as a distinguishing mark of Christians the fact that they have a future: it is not that they know the details of what awaits them, but they know in general terms that their life will not end in emptiness. Only when the future is certain as a positive reality does it become possible to live the present as well. So now we can say: Christian-

ity was not only "good news"—the communication of a hitherto unknown content. In our language we would say: the Christian message was not only "informative" but "performative." That means: the Gospel is not merely a communication of things that can be known—it is one that makes things happen and is life-changing. The dark door of time, of the future, has been thrown open. The one who has hope lives differently; the one who hopes has been granted the gift of a new life.

3. Yet at this point a question arises: in what does this hope consist which, as hope, is "redemption"? The essence of the answer is given in the phrase from the *Letter to the Ephesians* quoted above: the Ephesians, before their encounter with Christ, were without hope because they were "without God in the world." To come to know God—the true God—means to receive hope. We who have always lived with the Christian concept of God, and have grown accustomed to it, have almost ceased to notice that we possess the hope that ensues from a real encounter with this God. The example of a saint of our time can to some degree help us understand what it means to have a real encounter with this God for the first time. I am thinking of the African Josephine Bakhita, canonized by Pope John Paul II. She was born around 1869—she herself did not know the precise date—in Darfur in Sudan. At the age of nine, she was kidnapped by slave-traders, beaten till she bled, and sold five times in the slave-markets of Sudan. Eventually she found herself working as a slave for the mother and the wife of a general, and there she was flogged every day till she bled; as a result of this she bore 144 scars throughout her life. Finally, in 1882, she was bought by an Italian merchant for the Italian consul Callisto Legnani, who returned to Italy as the Mahdists advanced. Here, after the terrifying "masters" who had owned her up to that point, Bakhita came to know a totally different kind of "master"—in Venetian dialect, which she

was now learning, she used the name "*paron*" for the living God, the God of Jesus Christ. Up to that time she had known only masters who despised and maltreated her, or at best considered her a useful slave. Now, however, she heard that there is a "*paron*" above all masters, the Lord of all lords, and that this Lord is good, goodness in person. She came to know that this Lord even knew her, that he had created her—that he actually loved her. She too was loved, and by none other than the supreme "*Paron*," before whom all other masters are themselves no more than lowly servants. She was known and loved and she was awaited. What is more, this master had himself accepted the destiny of being flogged and now he was waiting for her "at the Father's right hand." Now she had "hope"—no longer simply the modest hope of finding masters who would be less cruel, but the great hope: "I am definitively loved and whatever happens to me—I am awaited by this Love. And so my life is good." Through the knowledge of this hope she was "redeemed," no longer a slave, but a free child of God. She understood what Paul meant when he reminded the Ephesians that previously they were without hope and without God in the world—without hope *because* without God. Hence, when she was about to be taken back to Sudan, Bakhita refused; she did not wish to be separated again from her "*Paron*." On 9 January 1890, she was baptized and confirmed and received her first Holy Communion from the hands of the Patriarch of Venice. On 8 December 1896, in Verona, she took her vows in the Congregation of the Canossian Sisters and from that time onwards, besides her work in the sacristy and in the porter's lodge at the convent, she made several journeys round Italy in order to promote the missions: the liberation that she had received through her encounter with the God of Jesus Christ, she felt she had to extend, it had to be handed on to others, to the greatest possible number of people. The hope born in her which had "redeemed" her she could not keep to herself; this hope had to reach many, to reach everybody.

4

The concept of faith-based hope in the New Testament and the early Church

4. We have raised the question: can our encounter with the God who in Christ has shown us his face and opened his heart be for us too not just "informative" but "performative"—that is to say, can it change our lives, so that we know we are redeemed through the hope that it expresses? Before attempting to answer the question, let us return once more to the early Church. It is not difficult to realize that the experience of the African slave-girl Bakhita was also the experience of many in the period of nascent Christianity who were beaten and condemned to slavery. Christianity did not bring a message of social revolution like that of the ill-fated Spartacus, whose struggle led to so much bloodshed. Jesus was not Spartacus, he was not engaged in a fight for political liberation like Barabbas or Bar-Kochba. Jesus, who himself died on the Cross, brought something totally different: an encounter with the Lord of all lords, an encounter with the living God and thus an encounter with a hope stronger than the sufferings of slavery, a hope which therefore transformed life and the world from within. What was new here can be seen with the utmost clarity in Saint Paul's *Letter to Philemon*. This is a very personal letter, which Paul wrote from prison and entrusted to the runaway slave Onesimus for his master, Philemon. Yes, Paul is sending the slave back to the master from whom he had fled, not ordering but asking: "I appeal to you for my child . . . whose father I have become in my imprisonment . . . I am sending him back to you, sending my very heart . . . perhaps this is why he was parted from you for a while, that you might have him back for ever, no longer as a slave but more than a slave, as a beloved brother . . ." (*Philem* 10-16). Those who, as far as their civil status is concerned, stand in

5

relation to one another as masters and slaves, inasmuch as they are members of the one Church have become brothers and sisters—this is how Christians addressed one another. By virtue of their Baptism they had been reborn, they had been given to drink of the same Spirit and they received the Body of the Lord together, alongside one another. Even if external structures remained unaltered, this changed society from within. When the *Letter to the Hebrews* says that Christians here on earth do not have a permanent homeland, but seek one which lies in the future (cf. *Heb* 11:13-16; *Phil* 3:20), this does not mean for one moment that they live only for the future: present society is recognized by Christians as an exile; they belong to a new society which is the goal of their common pilgrimage and which is anticipated in the course of that pilgrimage.

5. We must add a further point of view. The *First Letter to the Corinthians* (1:18-31) tells us that many of the early Christians belonged to the lower social strata, and precisely for this reason were open to the experience of new hope, as we saw in the example of Bakhita. Yet from the beginning there were also conversions in the aristocratic and cultured circles, since they too were living "without hope and without God in the world." Myth had lost its credibility; the Roman State religion had become fossilized into simple ceremony which was scrupulously carried out, but by then it was merely "political religion." Philosophical rationalism had confined the gods within the realm of unreality. The Divine was seen in various ways in cosmic forces, but a God to whom one could pray did not exist. Paul illustrates the essential problem of the religion of that time quite accurately when he contrasts life "according to Christ" with life under the dominion of the "elemental spirits of the universe" (*Col* 2:8). In this regard a text by Saint Gregory Nazianzen is enlightening. He says that at the very moment when the Magi, guided by the star, adored Christ the new king, astrology

6

came to an end, because the stars were now moving in the orbit determined by Christ.[2] This scene, in fact, overturns the worldview of that time, which in a different way has become fashionable once again today. It is not the elemental spirits of the universe, the laws of matter, which ultimately govern the world and mankind, but a personal God governs the stars, that is, the universe; it is not the laws of matter and of evolution that have the final say, but reason, will, love—a Person. And if we know this Person and he knows us, then truly the inexorable power of material elements no longer has the last word; we are not slaves of the universe and of its laws, we are free. In ancient times, honest enquiring minds were aware of this. Heaven is not empty. Life is not a simple product of laws and the randomness of matter, but within everything and at the same time above everything, there is a personal will, there is a Spirit who in Jesus has revealed himself as Love.[3]

6. The sarcophagi of the early Christian era illustrate this concept visually—in the context of death, in the face of which the question concerning life's meaning becomes unavoidable. The figure of Christ is interpreted on ancient sarcophagi principally by two images: the philosopher and the shepherd. Philosophy at that time was not generally seen as a difficult academic discipline, as it is today. Rather, the philosopher was someone who knew how to teach the essential art: the art of being authentically human—the art of living and dying. To be sure, it had long since been realized that many of the people who went around pretending to be philosophers, teachers of life, were just charlatans who made money through their words, while having nothing to say about real life. All the more, then, the true philosopher who really did know how to point out the path of life was highly sought after. Towards the end of the third century, on the sarcophagus of a child in Rome, we find for the first time, in the context of the resurrection of Lazarus, the

figure of Christ as the true philosopher, holding the Gospel in one hand and the philosopher's traveling staff in the other. With his staff, he conquers death; the Gospel brings the truth that itinerant philosophers had searched for in vain. In this image, which then became a common feature of sarcophagus art for a long time, we see clearly what both educated and simple people found in Christ: he tells us who man truly is and what a man must do in order to be truly human. He shows us the way, and this way is the truth. He himself is both the way and the truth, and therefore he is also the life which all of us are seeking. He also shows us the way beyond death; only someone able to do this is a true teacher of life. The same thing becomes visible in the image of the shepherd. As in the representation of the philosopher, so too through the figure of the shepherd the early Church could identify with existing models of Roman art. There the shepherd was generally an expression of the dream of a tranquil and simple life, for which the people, amid the confusion of the big cities, felt a certain longing. Now the image was read as part of a new scenario which gave it a deeper content: "The Lord is my shepherd: I shall not want . . . Even though I walk through the valley of the shadow of death, I fear no evil, because you are with me . . ." (*Ps* 23 [22]:1, 4). The true shepherd is one who knows even the path that passes through the valley of death; one who walks with me even on the path of final solitude, where no one can accompany me, guiding me through: he himself has walked this path, he has descended into the kingdom of death, he has conquered death, and he has returned to accompany us now and to give us the certainty that, together with him, we can find a way through. The realization that there is One who even in death accompanies me, and with his "rod and his staff comforts me," so that "I fear no evil" (cf. *Ps* 23 [22]:4)—this was the new "hope" that arose over the life of believers.

7. We must return once more to the New Testament. In the eleventh chapter of the *Letter to the Hebrews* (v. 1) we find a kind of definition of faith which closely links this virtue with hope. Ever since the Reformation there has been a dispute among exegetes over the central word of this phrase, but today a way towards a common interpretation seems to be opening up once more. For the time being I shall leave this central word untranslated. The sentence therefore reads as follows: "Faith is the *hypostasis* of things hoped for; the proof of things not seen." For the Fathers and for the theologians of the Middle Ages, it was clear that the Greek word *hypostasis* was to be rendered in Latin with the term *substantia*. The Latin translation of the text produced at the time of the early Church therefore reads: *Est autem fides sperandarum substantia rerum, argumentum non apparentium*—faith is the "substance" of things hoped for; the proof of things not seen. Saint Thomas Aquinas,[4] using the terminology of the philosophical tradition to which he belonged, explains it as follows: faith is a *habitus*, that is, a stable disposition of the spirit, through which eternal life takes root in us, and reason is led to consent to what it does not see. The concept of "substance" is therefore modified in the sense that through faith, in a tentative way, or as we might say "in embryo"—and thus according to the "substance"—there are already present in us the things that are hoped for: the whole, true life. And precisely because the thing itself is already present, this presence of what is to come also creates certainty: this "thing" which must come is not yet visible in the external world (it does not "appear"), but because of the fact that, as an initial and dynamic reality, we carry it within us, a certain perception of it has even now come into existence. To Luther, who was not particularly fond of the *Letter to the Hebrews*, the concept of "substance," in the context of his view of faith, meant nothing. For this reason he understood the term *hypostasis/substance* not in the objective

sense (of a reality present within us), but in the subjective sense, as an expression of an interior attitude, and so, naturally, he also had to understand the term *argumentum* as a disposition of the subject. In the twentieth century this interpretation became prevalent—at least in Germany—in Catholic exegesis too, so that the ecumenical translation into German of the New Testament, approved by the Bishops, reads as follows: *Glaube aber ist: Feststehen in dem, was man erhofft, Überzeugtsein von dem, was man nicht sieht* (faith is: standing firm in what one hopes, being convinced of what one does not see). This in itself is not incorrect, but it is not the meaning of the text, because the Greek term used (*elenchos*) does not have the subjective sense of "conviction" but the objective sense of "proof." Rightly, therefore, recent Protestant exegesis has arrived at a different interpretation: "Yet there can be no question but that this classical Protestant understanding is untenable."[5] Faith is not merely a personal reaching out towards things to come that are still totally absent: it gives us something. It gives us even now something of the reality we are waiting for, and this present reality constitutes for us a "proof" of the things that are still unseen. Faith draws the future into the present, so that it is no longer simply a "not yet." The fact that this future exists changes the present; the present is touched by the future reality, and thus the things of the future spill over into those of the present and those of the present into those of the future.

8. This explanation is further strengthened and related to daily life if we consider verse 34 of the tenth chapter of the *Letter to the Hebrews*, which is linked by vocabulary and content to this definition of hope-filled faith and prepares the way for it. Here the author speaks to believers who have undergone the experience of persecution, and he says to them: "you had compassion on the prisoners, and you joyfully accepted the plundering of your property (*hyparchonton*—Vulgate *bonorum*), since you knew that

10

you yourselves had a better possession (*hyparxin*—Vulgate *substantiam*) and an abiding one." *Hyparchonta* refers to property, to what in earthly life constitutes the means of support, indeed the basis, the "substance" for life, what we depend upon. This "substance," life's normal source of security, has been taken away from Christians in the course of persecution. They have stood firm, though, because they considered this material substance to be of little account. They could abandon it because they had found a better "basis" for their existence—a basis that abides, that no one can take away. We must not overlook the link between these two types of "substance," between means of support or material basis and the word of faith as the "basis," the "substance" that endures. Faith gives life a new basis, a new foundation on which we can stand, one which relativizes the habitual foundation, the reliability of material income. A new freedom is created with regard to this habitual foundation of life, which only *appears* to be capable of providing support, although this is obviously not to deny its normal meaning. This new freedom, the awareness of the new "substance" which we have been given, is revealed not only in martyrdom, in which people resist the overbearing power of ideology and its political organs and, by their death, renew the world. Above all, it is seen in the great acts of renunciation, from the monks of ancient times to Saint Francis of Assisi and those of our contemporaries who enter modern religious institutes and movements and leave everything for love of Christ, so as to bring to men and women the faith and love of Christ, and to help those who are suffering in body and spirit. In their case, the new "substance" has proved to be a genuine "substance"; from the hope of these people who have been touched by Christ, hope has arisen for others who were living in darkness and without hope. In their case, it has been demonstrated that this new life truly possesses and is "substance" that calls forth life for others. For us who contemplate these figures, their way of acting and living is *de facto* a "proof" that the things to come, the promise of Christ, are not

11

only a reality that we await, but a real presence: he is truly the "philosopher" and the "shepherd" who shows us what life is and where it is to be found.

9. In order to understand more deeply this reflection on the two types of substance—*hypostasis* and *hyparchonta*—and on the two approaches to life expressed by these terms, we must continue with a brief consideration of two words pertinent to the discussion which can be found in the tenth chapter of the *Letter to the Hebrews*. I refer to the words *hypomone* (10:36) and *hypostole* (10:39). *Hypomone* is normally translated as "patience"—perseverance, constancy. Knowing how to wait, while patiently enduring trials, is necessary for the believer to be able to "receive what is promised" (10:36). In the religious context of ancient Judaism, this word was used expressly for the expectation of God which was characteristic of Israel, for their persevering faithfulness to God on the basis of the certainty of the Covenant in a world which contradicts God. Thus the word indicates a lived hope, a life based on the certainty of hope. In the New Testament this expectation of God, this standing with God, takes on a new significance: in Christ, God has revealed himself. He has already communicated to us the "substance" of things to come, and thus the expectation of God acquires a new certainty. It is the expectation of things to come from the perspective of a present that is already given. It is a looking-forward in Christ's presence, with Christ who is present, to the perfecting of his Body, to his definitive coming. The word *hypostole*, on the other hand, means shrinking back through lack of courage to speak openly and frankly a truth that may be dangerous. Hiding through a spirit of fear leads to "destruction" (*Heb* 10:39). "God did not give us a spirit of timidity but a spirit of power and love and self-control"—that, by contrast, is the beautiful way in which the *Second Letter to Timothy* (1:7) describes the fundamental attitude of the Christian.

Eternal life—what is it?

10. We have spoken thus far of faith and hope in the New Testament and in early Christianity; yet it has always been clear that we are referring not only to the past: the entire reflection concerns living and dying in general, and therefore it also concerns us here and now. So now we must ask explicitly: is the Christian faith also for us today a life-changing and life-sustaining hope? Is it "performative" for us—is it a message which shapes our life in a new way, or is it just "information" which, in the meantime, we have set aside and which now seems to us to have been superseded by more recent information? In the search for an answer, I would like to begin with the classical form of the dialogue with which the rite of Baptism expressed the reception of an infant into the community of believers and the infant's rebirth in Christ. First of all the priest asked what name the parents had chosen for the child, and then he continued with the question: "What do you ask of the Church?" Answer: "Faith." "And what does faith give you?" "Eternal life." According to this dialogue, the parents were seeking access to the faith for their child, communion with believers, because they saw in faith the key to "eternal life." Today as in the past, this is what being baptized, becoming Christians, is all about: it is not just an act of socialization within the community, not simply a welcome into the Church. The parents expect more for the one to be baptized: they expect that faith, which includes the corporeal nature of the Church and her sacraments, will give life to their child—eternal life. Faith is the substance of hope. But then the question arises: do we really want this—to live eternally? Perhaps many people reject the faith today simply because they do not find the prospect of eternal life attractive. What they desire is not eternal life at all, but this present life, for which faith in eternal life seems something of an impediment. To continue living

forever—endlessly—appears more like a curse than a gift. Death, admittedly, one would wish to postpone for as long as possible. But to live always, without end—this, all things considered, can only be monotonous and ultimately unbearable. This is precisely the point made, for example, by Saint Ambrose, one of the Church Fathers, in the funeral discourse for his deceased brother Satyrus: "Death was not part of nature; it became part of nature. God did not decree death from the beginning; he prescribed it as a remedy. Human life, because of sin . . . began to experience the burden of wretchedness in unremitting labor and unbearable sorrow. There had to be a limit to its evils; death had to restore what life had forfeited. Without the assistance of grace, immortality is more of a burden than a blessing."[6] A little earlier, Ambrose had said: "Death is, then, no cause for mourning, for it is the cause of mankind's salvation."[7]

11. Whatever precisely Saint Ambrose may have meant by these words, it is true that to eliminate death or to postpone it more or less indefinitely would place the earth and humanity in an impossible situation, and even for the individual would bring no benefit. Obviously there is a contradiction in our attitude, which points to an inner contradiction in our very existence. On the one hand, we do not want to die; above all, those who love us do not want us to die. Yet on the other hand, neither do we want to continue living indefinitely, nor was the earth created with that in view. So what do we really want? Our paradoxical attitude gives rise to a deeper question: what in fact is "life"? And what does "eternity" really mean? There are moments when it suddenly seems clear to us: yes, this is what true "life" is—this is what it should be like. Besides, what we call "life" in our everyday language is not real "life" at all. Saint Augustine, in the extended letter on prayer which he addressed to Proba, a wealthy Roman widow and mother of three

consuls, once wrote this: ultimately we want only one thing—"the blessed life," the life which is simply life, simply "happiness." In the final analysis, there is nothing else that we ask for in prayer. Our journey has no other goal—it is about this alone. But then Augustine also says: looking more closely, we have no idea what we ultimately desire, what we would really like. We do not know this reality at all; even in those moments when we think we can reach out and touch it, it eludes us. "We do not know what we should pray for as we ought," he says, quoting Saint Paul (*Rom* 8:26). All we know is that it is not this. Yet in not knowing, we know that this reality must exist. "There is therefore in us a certain learned ignorance (*docta ignorantia*), so to speak," he writes. We do not know what we would really like; we do not know this "true life"; and yet we know that there must be something we do not know towards which we feel driven.[8]

12. I think that in this very precise and permanently valid way, Augustine is describing man's essential situation, the situation that gives rise to all his contradictions and hopes. In some way we want life itself, true life, untouched even by death; yet at the same time we do not know the thing towards which we feel driven. We cannot stop reaching out for it, and yet we know that all we can experience or accomplish is not what we yearn for. This unknown "thing" is the true "hope" which drives us, and at the same time the fact that it is unknown is the cause of all forms of despair and also of all efforts, whether positive or destructive, directed towards worldly authenticity and human authenticity. The term "eternal life" is intended to give a name to this known "unknown." Inevitably it is an inadequate term that creates confusion. "Eternal," in fact, suggests to us the idea of something interminable, and this frightens us; "life" makes us think of the life that we know and love and do not want to lose, even though very often it brings more

15

toil than satisfaction, so that while on the one hand we desire it, on the other hand we do not want it. To imagine ourselves outside the temporality that imprisons us and in some way to sense that eternity is not an unending succession of days in the calendar, but something more like the supreme moment of satisfaction, in which totality embraces us and we embrace totality—this we can only attempt. It would be like plunging into the ocean of infinite love, a moment in which time—the before and after—no longer exists. We can only attempt to grasp the idea that such a moment is life in the full sense, a plunging ever anew into the vastness of being, in which we are simply overwhelmed with joy. This is how Jesus expresses it in Saint John's Gospel: "I will see you again and your hearts will rejoice, and no one will take your joy from you" (16:22). We must think along these lines if we want to understand the object of Christian hope, to understand what it is that our faith, our being with Christ, leads us to expect.[9]

Is Christian hope individualistic?

13. In the course of their history, Christians have tried to express this "knowing without knowing" by means of figures that can be represented, and they have developed images of "Heaven" which remain far removed from what, after all, can only be known negatively, via unknowing. All these attempts at the representation of hope have given to many people, down the centuries, the incentive to live by faith and hence also to abandon their *hyparchonta*, the material substance for their lives. The author of the *Letter to the Hebrews*, in the eleventh chapter, outlined a kind of history of those who live in hope and of their journeying, a history which stretches from the time of Abel into the author's own day. This type of hope has been subjected to an increasingly harsh critique in modern times: it is dismissed as pure individualism, a way of abandoning the world to its misery and taking refuge in a private form of eternal salvation. Henri de Lubac, in the introduction to his seminal book *Catholicisme. Aspects sociaux du dogme*, assembled some characteristic articulations of this viewpoint, one of which is worth quoting: "Should I have found joy? No . . . only *my* joy, and that is something wildly different. . . . The joy of Jesus can be personal. It can belong to a single man and he is saved. He is at peace . . . now and always, but he is alone. The isolation of this joy does not trouble him. On the contrary: he is the chosen one! In his blessedness he passes through the battlefields with a rose in his hand."[10]

14. Against this, drawing upon the vast range of patristic theology, de Lubac was able to demonstrate that salvation has always been considered a "social" reality. Indeed, the *Letter to the Hebrews* speaks of a "city" (cf. 11:10, 16; 12:22; 13:14) and therefore of communal salvation. Consistently with this view, sin is understood

17

by the Fathers as the destruction of the unity of the human race, as fragmentation and division. Babel, the place where languages were confused, the place of separation, is seen to be an expression of what sin fundamentally is. Hence "redemption" appears as the re-establishment of unity, in which we come together once more in a union that begins to take shape in the world community of believers. We need not concern ourselves here with all the texts in which the social character of hope appears. Let us concentrate on the *Letter to Proba* in which Augustine tries to illustrate to some degree this "known unknown" that we seek. His point of departure is simply the expression "blessed life." Then he quotes *Psalm* 144 [143]:15: "Blessed is the people whose God is the Lord." And he continues: "In order to be numbered among this people and attain to . . . everlasting life with God, 'the end of the commandment is charity that issues from a pure heart and a good conscience and sincere faith' (*1 Tim* 1:5)."[11] This real life, towards which we try to reach out again and again, is linked to a lived union with a "people," and for each individual it can only be attained within this "we." It presupposes that we escape from the prison of our "I," because only in the openness of this universal subject does our gaze open out to the source of joy, to love itself—to God.

15. While this community-oriented vision of the "blessed life" is certainly directed beyond the present world, as such it also has to do with the building up of this world—in very different ways, according to the historical context and the possibilities offered or excluded thereby. At the time of Augustine, the incursions of new peoples were threatening the cohesion of the world, where hitherto there had been a certain guarantee of law and of living in a juridically ordered society; at that time, then, it was a matter of strengthening the basic foundations of this peaceful societal exis-

tence, in order to survive in a changed world. Let us now consider a more or less randomly chosen episode from the Middle Ages, that serves in many respects to illustrate what we have been saying. It was commonly thought that monasteries were places of flight from the world (*contemptus mundi*) and of withdrawal from responsibility for the world, in search of private salvation. Bernard of Clairvaux, who inspired a multitude of young people to enter the monasteries of his reformed Order, had quite a different perspective on this. In his view, monks perform a task for the whole Church and hence also for the world. He uses many images to illustrate the responsibility that monks have towards the entire body of the Church, and indeed towards humanity; he applies to them the words of pseudo-Rufinus: "The human race lives thanks to a few; were it not for them, the world would perish. . . ."[12] Contemplatives—*contemplantes*—must become agricultural laborers—*laborantes*—he says. The nobility of work, which Christianity inherited from Judaism, had already been expressed in the monastic rules of Augustine and Benedict. Bernard takes up this idea again. The young noblemen who flocked to his monasteries had to engage in manual labor. In fact Bernard explicitly states that not even the monastery can restore Paradise, but he maintains that, as a place of practical and spiritual "tilling the soil," it must prepare the new Paradise. A wild plot of forest land is rendered fertile—and in the process, the trees of pride are felled, whatever weeds may be growing inside souls are pulled up, and the ground is thereby prepared so that bread for body and soul can flourish.[13] Are we not perhaps seeing once again, in the light of current history, that no positive world order can prosper where souls are overgrown?

The transformation of Christian faith-hope in the modern age

16. How could the idea have developed that Jesus' message is narrowly individualistic and aimed only at each person singly? How did we arrive at this interpretation of the "salvation of the soul" as a flight from responsibility for the whole, and how did we come to conceive the Christian project as a selfish search for salvation which rejects the idea of serving others? In order to find an answer to this we must take a look at the foundations of the modern age. These appear with particular clarity in the thought of Francis Bacon. That a new era emerged—through the discovery of America and the new technical achievements that had made this development possible—is undeniable. But what is the basis of this new era? It is the new correlation of experiment and method that enables man to arrive at an interpretation of nature in conformity with its laws and thus finally to achieve "the triumph of art over nature" (*victoria cursus artis super naturam*).[14] The novelty—according to Bacon's vision—lies in a new correlation between science and praxis. This is also given a theological application: the new correlation between science and praxis would mean that the dominion over creation—given to man by God and lost through original sin—would be re-established.[15]

17. Anyone who reads and reflects on these statements attentively will recognize that a disturbing step has been taken: up to that time, the recovery of what man had lost through the expulsion from Paradise was expected from faith in Jesus Christ: herein lay "redemption." Now, this "redemption," the restoration of the lost "Paradise" is no longer expected from faith, but from the newly discovered link between science and praxis. It is not that faith is simply denied; rather it is displaced onto another level—that

of purely private and other-worldly affairs—and at the same time it becomes somehow irrelevant for the world. This programmatic vision has determined the trajectory of modern times and it also shapes the present-day crisis of faith which is essentially a crisis of Christian hope. Thus hope too, in Bacon, acquires a new form. Now it is called: *faith in progress*. For Bacon, it is clear that the recent spate of discoveries and inventions is just the beginning; through the interplay of science and praxis, totally new discoveries will follow, a totally new world will emerge, the kingdom of man.[16] He even put forward a vision of foreseeable inventions—including the airplane and the submarine. As the ideology of progress developed further, joy at visible advances in human potential remained a continuing confirmation of *faith in progress* as such.

18. At the same time, two categories become increasingly central to the idea of progress: reason and freedom. Progress is primarily associated with the growing dominion of reason, and this reason is obviously considered to be a force of good and a force for good. Progress is the overcoming of all forms of dependency—it is progress towards perfect freedom. Likewise freedom is seen purely as a promise, in which man becomes more and more fully himself. In both concepts—freedom and reason—there is a political aspect. The kingdom of reason, in fact, is expected as the new condition of the human race once it has attained total freedom. The political conditions of such a kingdom of reason and freedom, however, appear at first sight somewhat ill defined. Reason and freedom seem to guarantee by themselves, by virtue of their intrinsic goodness, a new and perfect human community. The two key concepts of "reason" and "freedom," however, were tacitly interpreted as being in conflict with the shackles of faith and of the Church as well as those of the political structures of the period. Both concepts therefore contain a revolutionary potential of enormous explosive force.

19. We must look briefly at the two essential stages in the political realization of this hope, because they are of great importance for the development of Christian hope, for a proper understanding of it and of the reasons for its persistence. First there is the French Revolution—an attempt to establish the rule of reason and freedom as a political reality. To begin with, the Europe of the Enlightenment looked on with fascination at these events, but then, as they developed, had cause to reflect anew on reason and freedom. A good illustration of these two phases in the reception of events in France is found in two essays by Immanuel Kant in which he reflects on what had taken place. In 1792 he wrote *Der Sieg des guten Prinzips über das böse und die Gründung eines Reiches Gottes auf Erden* ("The Victory of the Good over the Evil Principle and the Founding of a Kingdom of God on Earth"). In this text he says the following: "The gradual transition of ecclesiastical faith to the exclusive sovereignty of pure religious faith is the coming of the Kingdom of God."[17] He also tells us that revolutions can accelerate this transition from ecclesiastical faith to rational faith. The "Kingdom of God" proclaimed by Jesus receives a new definition here and takes on a new mode of presence; a new "imminent expectation," so to speak, comes into existence: the "Kingdom of God" arrives where "ecclesiastical faith" is vanquished and superseded by "religious faith," that is to say, by simple rational faith. In 1795, in the text *Das Ende aller Dinge* ("The End of All Things") a changed image appears. Now Kant considers the possibility that as well as the natural end of all things there may be another that is unnatural, a perverse end. He writes in this connection: "If Christianity should one day cease to be worthy of love . . . then the prevailing mode in human thought would be rejection and opposition to it; and the Antichrist . . . would begin his—albeit short—regime (presumably based on fear and self-interest); but then, because Christianity, though destined to be the world religion, would not in fact be favored by destiny to become so, then, in a moral respect, this could lead to the (perverted) end of all things."[18]

22

20. The nineteenth century held fast to its faith in progress as the new form of human hope, and it continued to consider reason and freedom as the guiding stars to be followed along the path of hope. Nevertheless, the increasingly rapid advance of technical development and the industrialization connected with it soon gave rise to an entirely new social situation: there emerged a class of industrial workers and the so-called "industrial proletariat," whose dreadful living conditions Friedrich Engels described alarmingly in 1845. For his readers, the conclusion is clear: this cannot continue; a change is necessary. Yet the change would shake up and overturn the entire structure of bourgeois society. After the bourgeois revolution of 1789, the time had come for a new, proletarian revolution: progress could not simply continue in small, linear steps. A revolutionary leap was needed. Karl Marx took up the rallying call, and applied his incisive language and intellect to the task of launching this major new and, as he thought, definitive step in history towards salvation—towards what Kant had described as the "Kingdom of God." Once the truth of the hereafter had been rejected, it would then be a question of establishing the truth of the here and now. The critique of Heaven is transformed into the critique of earth, the critique of theology into the critique of politics. Progress towards the better, towards the definitively good world, no longer comes simply from science but from politics—from a scientifically conceived politics that recognizes the structure of history and society and thus points out the road towards revolution, towards all-encompassing change. With great precision, albeit with a certain one-sided bias, Marx described the situation of his time, and with great analytical skill he spelled out the paths leading to revolution—and not only theoretically: by means of the Communist Party that came into being from the Communist Manifesto of 1848, he set it in motion. His promise, owing to the acuteness of his analysis and his clear indication of the means for

radical change, was and still remains an endless source of fascination. Real revolution followed, in the most radical way in Russia.

21. Together with the victory of the revolution, though, Marx's fundamental error also became evident. He showed precisely how to overthrow the existing order, but he did not say how matters should proceed thereafter. He simply presumed that with the expropriation of the ruling class, with the fall of political power and the socialization of means of production, the new Jerusalem would be realized. Then, indeed, all contradictions would be resolved, man and the world would finally sort themselves out. Then everything would be able to proceed by itself along the right path, because everything would belong to everyone and all would desire the best for one another. Thus, having accomplished the revolution, Lenin must have realized that the writings of the master gave no indication as to how to proceed. True, Marx had spoken of the interim phase of the dictatorship of the proletariat as a necessity which in time would automatically become redundant. This "intermediate phase" we know all too well, and we also know how it then developed, not ushering in a perfect world, but leaving behind a trail of appalling destruction. Marx not only omitted to work out how this new world would be organized—which should, of course, have been unnecessary. His silence on this matter follows logically from his chosen approach. His error lay deeper. He forgot that man always remains man. He forgot man and he forgot man's freedom. He forgot that freedom always remains also freedom for evil. He thought that once the economy had been put right, everything would automatically be put right. His real error is materialism: man, in fact, is not merely the product of economic conditions, and it is not possible to redeem him purely from the outside by creating a favorable economic environment.

22. Again, we find ourselves facing the question: what may we hope? A self-critique of modernity is needed in dialogue with Christianity and its concept of hope. In this dialogue Christians too, in the context of their knowledge and experience, must learn anew in what their hope truly consists, what they have to offer to the world and what they cannot offer. Flowing into this self-critique of the modern age there also has to be a self-critique of modern Christianity, which must constantly renew its self-understanding setting out from its roots. On this subject, all we can attempt here are a few brief observations. First we must ask ourselves: what does "progress" really mean; what does it promise and what does it not promise? In the nineteenth century, faith in progress was already subject to critique. In the twentieth century, Theodor W. Adorno formulated the problem of faith in progress quite drastically: he said that progress, seen accurately, is progress from the sling to the atom bomb. Now this is certainly an aspect of progress that must not be concealed. To put it another way: the ambiguity of progress becomes evident. Without doubt, it offers new possibilities for good, but it also opens up appalling possibilities for evil—possibilities that formerly did not exist. We have all witnessed the way in which progress, in the wrong hands, can become and has indeed become a terrifying progress in evil. If technical progress is not matched by corresponding progress in man's ethical formation, in man's inner growth (cf. *Eph* 3:16; *2 Cor* 4:16), then it is not progress at all, but a threat for man and for the world.

23. As far as the two great themes of "reason" and "freedom" are concerned, here we can only touch upon the issues connected with them. Yes indeed, reason is God's great gift to man, and the victory of reason over unreason is also a goal of the Christian life. But when does reason truly triumph? When it is detached from God? When it has become blind to God? Is the reason behind action and capacity for action the whole of reason? If progress, in

order to be progress, needs moral growth on the part of humanity, then the reason behind action and capacity for action is likewise urgently in need of integration through reason's openness to the saving forces of faith, to the differentiation between good and evil. Only thus does reason become truly human. It becomes human only if it is capable of directing the will along the right path, and it is capable of this only if it looks beyond itself. Otherwise, man's situation, in view of the imbalance between his material capacity and the lack of judgment in his heart, becomes a threat for him and for creation. Thus where freedom is concerned, we must remember that human freedom always requires a convergence of various freedoms. Yet this convergence cannot succeed unless it is determined by a common intrinsic criterion of measurement, which is the foundation and goal of our freedom. Let us put it very simply: man needs God, otherwise he remains without hope. Given the developments of the modern age, the quotation from Saint Paul with which I began (*Eph* 2:12) proves to be thoroughly realistic and plainly true. There is no doubt, therefore, that a "Kingdom of God" accomplished without God—a kingdom therefore of man alone—inevitably ends up as the "perverse end" of all things as described by Kant: we have seen it, and we see it over and over again. Yet neither is there any doubt that God truly enters into human affairs only when, rather than being present merely in our thinking, he himself comes towards us and speaks to us. Reason therefore needs faith if it is to be completely itself: reason and faith need one another in order to fulfill their true nature and their mission.

The true shape of Christian hope

24. Let us ask once again: what may we hope? And what may we not hope? First of all, we must acknowledge that incremental progress is possible only in the material sphere. Here, amid our growing knowledge of the structure of matter and in the light of ever more advanced inventions, we clearly see continuous progress towards an ever greater mastery of nature. Yet in the field of ethical awareness and moral decision-making, there is no similar possibility of accumulation for the simple reason that man's freedom is always new and he must always make his decisions anew. These decisions can never simply be made for us in advance by others—if that were the case, we would no longer be free. Freedom presupposes that in fundamental decisions, every person and every generation is a new beginning. Naturally, new generations can build on the knowledge and experience of those who went before, and they can draw upon the moral treasury of the whole of humanity. But they can also reject it, because it can never be self-evident in the same way as material inventions. The moral treasury of humanity is not readily at hand like tools that we use; it is present as an appeal to freedom and a possibility for it. This, however, means that:

a.   The right state of human affairs, the moral well-being of the world can never be guaranteed simply through structures alone, however good they are. Such structures are not only important, but necessary; yet they cannot and must not marginalize human freedom. Even the best structures function only when the community is animated by convictions capable of motivating people to assent freely to the social order. Freedom requires conviction; conviction does not exist on its own, but must always be gained anew by the community.

b.   Since man always remains free and since his freedom is always
       fragile, the kingdom of good will never be definitively estab-
       lished in this world. Anyone who promises the better world
       that is guaranteed to last forever is making a false promise;
       he is overlooking human freedom. Freedom must constantly
       be won over for the cause of good. Free assent to the good
       never exists simply by itself. If there were structures which
       could irrevocably guarantee a determined—good—state of
       the world, man's freedom would be denied, and hence they
       would not be good structures at all.

25. What this means is that every generation has the task of engag-
ing anew in the arduous search for the right way to order human
affairs; this task is never simply completed. Yet every generation
must also make its own contribution to establishing convincing
structures of freedom and of good, which can help the following
generation as a guideline for the proper use of human freedom;
hence, always within human limits, they provide a certain guarantee also for the future. In other words: good structures help, but
of themselves they are not enough. Man can never be redeemed
simply from outside. Francis Bacon and those who followed in the
intellectual current of modernity that he inspired were wrong to
believe that man would be redeemed through science. Such an
expectation asks too much of science; this kind of hope is decep-
tive. Science can contribute greatly to making the world and mankind more human. Yet it can also destroy mankind and the world
unless it is steered by forces that lie outside it. On the other hand,
we must also acknowledge that modern Christianity, faced with
the successes of science in progressively structuring the world, has
to a large extent restricted its attention to the individual and his
salvation. In so doing it has limited the horizon of its hope and has
failed to recognize sufficiently the greatness of its task—even if it

has continued to achieve great things in the formation of man and in care for the weak and the suffering.

26. It is not science that redeems man: man is redeemed by love. This applies even in terms of this present world. When someone has the experience of a great love in his life, this is a moment of "redemption" which gives a new meaning to his life. But soon he will also realize that the love bestowed upon him cannot by itself resolve the question of his life. It is a love that remains fragile. It can be destroyed by death. The human being needs unconditional love. He needs the certainty which makes him say: "neither death, nor life, nor angels, nor principalities, nor things present, nor things to come, nor powers, nor height, nor depth, nor anything else in all creation, will be able to separate us from the love of God in Christ Jesus our Lord" (*Rom* 8:38-39). If this absolute love exists, with its absolute certainty, then—only then—is man "redeemed," whatever should happen to him in his particular circumstances. This is what it means to say: Jesus Christ has "redeemed" us. Through him we have become certain of God, a God who is not a remote "first cause" of the world, because his only-begotten Son has become man and of him everyone can say: "I live by faith in the Son of God, who loved me and gave himself for me" (*Gal* 2:20).

27. In this sense it is true that anyone who does not know God, even though he may entertain all kinds of hopes, is ultimately without hope, without the great hope that sustains the whole of life (cf. *Eph* 2:12). Man's great, true hope which holds firm in spite of all disappointments can only be God—God who has loved us and who continues to love us "to the end," until all "is accomplished" (cf. *Jn* 13:1 and 19:30). Whoever is moved by love begins to perceive what "life" really is. He begins to perceive the meaning

of the word of hope that we encountered in the Baptismal rite: from faith I await "eternal life"—the true life which, whole and unthreatened, in all its fullness, is simply life. Jesus, who said that he had come so that we might have life and have it in its fullness, in abundance (cf. *Jn* 10:10), has also explained to us what "life" means: "this is eternal life, that they know you the only true God, and Jesus Christ whom you have sent" (*Jn* 17:3). Life in its true sense is not something we have exclusively in or from ourselves: it is a relationship. And life in its totality is a relationship with him who is the source of life. If we are in relation with him who does not die, who is Life itself and Love itself, then we are in life. Then we "live."

28. Yet now the question arises: are we not in this way falling back once again into an individualistic understanding of salvation, into hope for myself alone, which is not true hope since it forgets and overlooks others? Indeed we are not! Our relationship with God is established through communion with Jesus—we cannot achieve it alone or from our own resources alone. The relationship with Jesus, however, is a relationship with the one who gave himself as a ransom for all (cf. *1 Tim* 2:6). Being in communion with Jesus Christ draws us into his "being for all"; it makes it our own way of being. He commits us to live for others, but only through communion with him does it become possible truly to be there for others, for the whole. In this regard I would like to quote the great Greek Doctor of the Church, Maximus the Confessor († 662), who begins by exhorting us to prefer nothing to the knowledge and love of God, but then quickly moves on to practicalities: "The one who loves God cannot hold on to money but rather gives it out in God's fashion . . . in the same manner in accordance with the measure of justice."[19] Love of God leads to participation in the justice and generosity of God towards others. Loving God requires

an interior freedom from all possessions and all material goods: the love of God is revealed in responsibility for others.[20] This same connection between love of God and responsibility for others can be seen in a striking way in the life of Saint Augustine. After his conversion to the Christian faith, he decided, together with some like-minded friends, to lead a life totally dedicated to the word of God and to things eternal. His intention was to practice a Christian version of the ideal of the contemplative life expressed in the great tradition of Greek philosophy, choosing in this way the "better part" (cf. *Lk* 10:42). Things turned out differently, however. While attending the Sunday liturgy at the port city of Hippo, he was called out from the assembly by the Bishop and constrained to receive ordination for the exercise of the priestly ministry in that city. Looking back on that moment, he writes in his *Confessions*: "Terrified by my sins and the weight of my misery, I had resolved in my heart, and meditated flight into the wilderness; but you forbade me and gave me strength, by saying: 'Christ died for all, that those who live might live no longer for themselves but for him who for their sake died' (cf. *2 Cor* 5:15)."[21] Christ died for all. To live for him means allowing oneself to be drawn into his *being for others*.

29. For Augustine this meant a totally new life. He once described his daily life in the following terms: "The turbulent have to be corrected, the faint-hearted cheered up, the weak supported; the Gospel's opponents need to be refuted, its insidious enemies guarded against; the unlearned need to be taught, the indolent stirred up, the argumentative checked; the proud must be put in their place, the desperate set on their feet, those engaged in quarrels reconciled; the needy have to be helped, the oppressed to be liberated, the good to be encouraged, the bad to be tolerated; all must be loved."[22] "The Gospel terrifies me"[23]—producing that healthy fear which prevents us from living for ourselves alone and

compels us to pass on the hope we hold in common. Amid the serious difficulties facing the Roman Empire—and also posing a serious threat to Roman Africa, which was actually destroyed at the end of Augustine's life—this was what he set out to do: to transmit hope, the hope which came to him from faith and which, in complete contrast with his introverted temperament, enabled him to take part decisively and with all his strength in the task of building up the city. In the same chapter of the *Confessions* in which we have just noted the decisive reason for his commitment "for all," he says that Christ "intercedes for us, otherwise I should despair. My weaknesses are many and grave, many and grave indeed, but more abundant still is your medicine. We might have thought that your word was far distant from union with man, and so we might have despaired of ourselves, if this Word had not become flesh and dwelt among us."[24] On the strength of his hope, Augustine dedicated himself completely to the ordinary people and to his city—renouncing his spiritual nobility, he preached and acted in a simple way for simple people.

30. Let us summarize what has emerged so far in the course of our reflections. Day by day, man experiences many greater or lesser hopes, different in kind according to the different periods of his life. Sometimes one of these hopes may appear to be totally satisfying without any need for other hopes. Young people can have the hope of a great and fully satisfying love; the hope of a certain position in their profession, or of some success that will prove decisive for the rest of their lives. When these hopes are fulfilled, however, it becomes clear that they were not, in reality, the whole. It becomes evident that man has need of a hope that goes further. It becomes clear that only something infinite will suffice for him, something that will always be more than he can ever attain. In this regard our contemporary age has developed the hope of creating a

perfect world that, thanks to scientific knowledge and to scientifically based politics, seemed to be achievable. Thus Biblical hope in the Kingdom of God has been displaced by hope in the kingdom of man, the hope of a better world which would be the real "Kingdom of God." This seemed at last to be the great and realistic hope that man needs. It was capable of galvanizing—for a time—all man's energies. The great objective seemed worthy of full commitment. In the course of time, however, it has become clear that this hope is constantly receding. Above all it has become apparent that this may be a hope for a future generation, but not for me. And however much "for all" may be part of the great hope—since I cannot be happy without others or in opposition to them—it remains true that a hope that does not concern me personally is not a real hope. It has also become clear that this hope is opposed to freedom, since human affairs depend in each generation on the free decisions of those concerned. If this freedom were to be taken away, as a result of certain conditions or structures, then ultimately this world would not be good, since a world without freedom can by no means be a good world. Hence, while we must always be committed to the improvement of the world, tomorrow's better world cannot be the proper and sufficient content of our hope. And in this regard the question always arises: when is the world "better"? What makes it good? By what standard are we to judge its goodness? What are the paths that lead to this "goodness"?

31. Let us say once again: we need the greater and lesser hopes that keep us going day by day. But these are not enough without the great hope, which must surpass everything else. This great hope can only be God, who encompasses the whole of reality and who can bestow upon us what we, by ourselves, cannot attain. The fact that it comes to us as a gift is actually part of hope. God is the foundation of hope: not any god, but the God who has a human

face and who has loved us to the end, each one of us and humanity in its entirety. His Kingdom is not an imaginary hereafter, situated in a future that will never arrive; his Kingdom is present wherever he is loved and wherever his love reaches us. His love alone gives us the possibility of soberly persevering day by day, without ceasing to be spurred on by hope, in a world which by its very nature is imperfect. His love is at the same time our guarantee of the existence of what we only vaguely sense and which nevertheless, in our deepest self, we await: a life that is "truly" life. Let us now, in the final section, develop this idea in more detail as we focus our attention on some of the "settings" in which we can learn in practice about hope and its exercise.

"Settings" for learning and practicing hope

I. Prayer as a school of hope

32. A first essential setting for learning hope is prayer. When no one listens to me any more, God still listens to me. When I can no longer talk to anyone or call upon anyone, I can always talk to God. When there is no longer anyone to help me deal with a need or expectation that goes beyond the human capacity for hope, he can help me.[25] When I have been plunged into complete solitude . . . ; if I pray I am never totally alone. The late Cardinal Nguyen Van Thuan, a prisoner for thirteen years, nine of them spent in solitary confinement, has left us a precious little book: *Prayers of Hope*. During thirteen years in jail, in a situation of seemingly utter hopelessness, the fact that he could listen and speak to God became for him an increasing power of hope, which enabled him, after his release, to become for people all over the world a witness to hope—to that great hope which does not wane even in the nights of solitude.

33. Saint Augustine, in a homily on the *First Letter of John*, describes very beautifully the intimate relationship between prayer and hope. He defines prayer as an exercise of desire. Man was created for greatness—for God himself; he was created to be filled by God. But his heart is too small for the greatness to which it is destined. It must be stretched. "By delaying [his gift], God strengthens our desire; through desire he enlarges our soul and by expanding it he increases its capacity [for receiving him]." Augustine refers to Saint Paul, who speaks of himself as straining forward to the things that are to come (cf. *Phil* 3:13). He then uses a very beautiful image to describe this process of enlargement and preparation

of the human heart. "Suppose that God wishes to fill you with honey [a symbol of God's tenderness and goodness]; but if you are full of vinegar, where will you put the honey?" The vessel, that is your heart, must first be enlarged and then cleansed, freed from the vinegar and its taste. This requires hard work and is painful, but in this way alone do we become suited to that for which we are destined.[26] Even if Augustine speaks directly only of our capacity for God, it is nevertheless clear that through this effort by which we are freed from vinegar and the taste of vinegar, not only are we made free for God, but we also become open to others. It is only by becoming children of God, that we can be with our common Father. To pray is not to step outside history and withdraw to our own private corner of happiness. When we pray properly we undergo a process of inner purification which opens us up to God and thus to our fellow human beings as well. In prayer we must learn what we can truly ask of God—what is worthy of God. We must learn that we cannot pray against others. We must learn that we cannot ask for the superficial and comfortable things that we desire at this moment—that meager, misplaced hope that leads us away from God. We must learn to purify our desires and our hopes. We must free ourselves from the hidden lies with which we deceive ourselves. God sees through them, and when we come before God, we too are forced to recognize them. "But who can discern his errors? Clear me from hidden faults," prays the Psalmist (Ps 19:12 [18:13]). Failure to recognize my guilt, the illusion of my innocence, does not justify me and does not save me, because I am culpable for the numbness of my conscience and my incapacity to recognize the evil in me for what it is. If God does not exist, perhaps I have to seek refuge in these lies, because there is no one who can forgive me, no one who is the true criterion. Yet my encounter with God awakens my conscience in such a way that it no longer aims at self-justification, and is no longer a mere reflection of me and those of my contemporaries who shape my thinking, but it becomes a capacity for listening to the Good itself.

34. For prayer to develop this power of purification, it must on the one hand be something very personal, an encounter between my intimate self and God, the living God. On the other hand it must be constantly guided and enlightened by the great prayers of the Church and of the saints, by liturgical prayer, in which the Lord teaches us again and again how to pray properly. Cardinal Nguyen Van Thuan, in his book of spiritual exercises, tells us that during his life there were long periods when he was unable to pray and that he would hold fast to the texts of the Church's prayer: the Our Father, the Hail Mary and the prayers of the liturgy.[27] Praying must always involve this intermingling of public and personal prayer. This is how we can speak to God and how God speaks to us. In this way we undergo those purifications by which we become open to God and are prepared for the service of our fellow human beings. We become capable of the great hope, and thus we become ministers of hope for others. Hope in a Christian sense is always hope for others as well. It is an active hope, in which we struggle to prevent things moving towards the "perverse end." It is an active hope also in the sense that we keep the world open to God. Only in this way does it continue to be a truly human hope.

II. Action and suffering as settings for learning hope

35. All serious and upright human conduct is hope in action. This is so first of all in the sense that we thereby strive to realize our lesser and greater hopes, to complete this or that task which is important for our onward journey, or we work towards a brighter and more humane world so as to open doors into the future. Yet our daily efforts in pursuing our own lives and in working for the

world's future either tire us or turn into fanaticism, unless we are enlightened by the radiance of the great hope that cannot be destroyed even by small-scale failures or by a breakdown in matters of historic importance. If we cannot hope for more than is effectively attainable at any given time, or more than is promised by political or economic authorities, our lives will soon be without hope. It is important to know that I can always continue to hope, even if in my own life, or the historical period in which I am living, there seems to be nothing left to hope for. Only the great certitude of hope that my own life and history in general, despite all failures, are held firm by the indestructible power of Love, and that this gives them their meaning and importance, only this kind of hope can then give the courage to act and to persevere. Certainly we cannot "build" the Kingdom of God by our own efforts—what we build will always be the kingdom of man with all the limitations proper to our human nature. The Kingdom of God is a gift, and precisely because of this, it is great and beautiful, and constitutes the response to our hope. And we cannot—to use the classical expression—"merit" Heaven through our works. Heaven is always more than we could merit, just as being loved is never something "merited," but always a gift. However, even when we are fully aware that Heaven far exceeds what we can merit, it will always be true that our behavior is not indifferent before God and therefore is not indifferent for the unfolding of history. We can open ourselves and the world and allow God to enter: we can open ourselves to truth, to love, to what is good. This is what the saints did, those who, as "God's fellow workers," contributed to the world's salvation (cf. 1 Cor 3:9; 1 Th 3:2). We can free our life and the world from the poisons and contaminations that could destroy the present and the future. We can uncover the sources of creation and keep them unsullied, and in this way we can make a right use of creation, which comes to us as a gift, according to its intrinsic requirements and ultimate purpose. This makes sense even if outwardly we achieve nothing or seem powerless in the face of overwhelming hostile forces. So on the one hand, our actions engender hope for us and for others; but at the same time, it is the great hope based upon God's promises that gives us courage and directs our action in good times and bad.

36. Like action, suffering is a part of our human existence. Suffering stems partly from our finitude, and partly from the mass of sin which has accumulated over the course of history, and continues to grow unabated today. Certainly we must do whatever we can to reduce suffering: to avoid as far as possible the suffering of the innocent; to soothe pain; to give assistance in overcoming mental suffering. These are obligations both in justice and in love, and they are included among the fundamental requirements of the Christian life and every truly human life. Great progress has been made in the battle against physical pain; yet the sufferings of the innocent and mental suffering have, if anything, increased in recent decades. Indeed, we must do all we can to overcome suffering, but to banish it from the world altogether is not in our power.

This is simply because we are unable to shake off our finitude and because none of us is capable of eliminating the power of evil, of sin which, as we plainly see, is a constant source of suffering. Only God is able to do this: only a God who personally enters history by making himself man and suffering within history. We know that this God exists, and hence that this power to "take away the sin of the world" (Jn 1:29) is present in the world. Through faith in the existence of this power, hope for the world's healing has emerged in history. It is, however, hope—not yet fulfillment; hope that gives us the courage to place ourselves on the side of good even in seemingly hopeless situations, aware that, as far as the external course of history is concerned, the power of sin will continue to be a terrible presence.

37. Let us return to our topic. We can try to limit suffering, to fight against it, but we cannot eliminate it. It is when we attempt to avoid suffering by withdrawing from anything that might involve hurt, when we try to spare ourselves the effort and pain of pursuing truth, love, and goodness, that we drift into a life of emptiness, in which there may be almost no pain, but the dark sensation of meaninglessness and abandonment is all the greater. It is not by sidestepping or fleeing from suffering that we are healed, but rather by our capacity for accepting it, maturing through it and finding meaning through union with Christ, who suffered with infinite love. In this context, I would like to quote a passage from a letter written by the Vietnamese martyr Paul Le-Bao-Tinh († 1857) which illustrates this transformation of suffering through the power of hope springing from faith. "I, Paul, in chains for the name of Christ, wish to relate to you the trials besetting me daily, in order that you may be inflamed with love for God and join with me in his praises, for his mercy is for ever (*Ps* 136 [135]). The prison here is a true image of everlasting Hell: to cruel tortures of every kind—shackles, iron chains, manacles—are added hatred, vengeance, calumnies, obscene speech, quarrels, evil acts, swearing, curses, as well as anguish and grief. But the God who once freed the three children from the fiery furnace is with me always; he has delivered me from these tribulations and made them sweet, for his mercy is for ever. In the midst of these torments, which usually terrify others, I am, by the grace of God, full of joy and gladness, because I am not alone—Christ is with me . . . How am I to bear with the spectacle, as each day I see emperors, mandarins, and their retinue blaspheming your holy name, O Lord, who are enthroned above the Cherubim and Seraphim? (cf. *Ps* 80:1 [79:2]). Behold, the pagans have trodden your Cross underfoot! Where is your glory? As I see all this, I would, in the ardent love I have for you, prefer to be torn limb from limb and to die as a witness to your love. O Lord, show your power, save me, sustain me,

that in my infirmity your power may be shown and may be glorified before the nations . . . Beloved brothers, as you hear all these things may you give endless thanks in joy to God, from whom every good proceeds; bless the Lord with me, for his mercy is for ever . . . I write these things to you in order that your faith and mine may be united. In the midst of this storm I cast my anchor towards the throne of God, the anchor that is the lively hope in my heart."[28] This is a letter from "Hell." It lays bare all the horror of a concentration camp, where to the torments inflicted by tyrants upon their victims is added the outbreak of evil in the victims themselves, such that they in turn become further instruments of their persecutors' cruelty. This is indeed a letter from Hell, but it also reveals the truth of the Psalm text: "If I go up to the heavens, you are there; if I sink to the nether world, you are present there . . . If I say, 'Surely the darkness shall hide me, and night shall be my light'—for you darkness itself is not dark, and night shines as the day; darkness and light are the same" (*Ps* 139 [138]:8-12; cf. also *Ps* 23 [22]:4). Christ descended into "Hell" and is therefore close to those cast into it, transforming their darkness into light. Suffering and torment is still terrible and well-nigh unbearable. Yet the star of hope has risen—the anchor of the heart reaches the very throne of God. Instead of evil being unleashed within man, the light shines victorious: suffering—without ceasing to be suffering—becomes, despite everything, a hymn of praise.

38. The true measure of humanity is essentially determined in relationship to suffering and to the sufferer. This holds true both for the individual and for society. A society unable to accept its suffering members and incapable of helping to share their suffering and to bear it inwardly through "com-passion" is a cruel and inhuman society. Yet society cannot accept its suffering members and support them in their trials unless individuals are capable of doing so themselves; moreover, the individual cannot accept another's

suffering unless he personally is able to find meaning in suffering, a path of purification and growth in maturity, a journey of hope. Indeed, to accept the "other" who suffers, means that I take up his suffering in such a way that it becomes mine also. Because it has now become a shared suffering, though, in which another person is present, this suffering is penetrated by the light of love. The Latin word *con-solatio*, "consolation," expresses this beautifully. It suggests *being with* the other in his solitude, so that it ceases to be solitude. Furthermore, the capacity to accept suffering for the sake of goodness, truth and justice is an essential criterion of humanity, because if my own well-being and safety are ultimately more important than truth and justice, then the power of the stronger prevails, then violence and untruth reign supreme. Truth and justice must stand above my comfort and physical well-being, or else my life itself becomes a lie. In the end, even the "yes" to love is a source of suffering, because love always requires expropriations of my "I," in which I allow myself to be pruned and wounded. Love simply cannot exist without this painful renunciation of myself, for otherwise it becomes pure selfishness and thereby ceases to be love.

39. To suffer with the other and for others; to suffer for the sake of truth and justice; to suffer out of love and in order to become a person who truly loves—these are fundamental elements of humanity, and to abandon them would destroy man himself. Yet once again the question arises: are we capable of this? Is the other important enough to warrant my becoming, on his account, a person who suffers? Does truth matter to me enough to make suffering worthwhile? Is the promise of love so great that it justifies the gift of myself? In the history of humanity, it was the Christian faith that had the particular merit of bringing forth within man a new and deeper capacity for these kinds of suffering that are decisive for his humanity. The Christian faith has shown us that truth, justice

and love are not simply ideals, but enormously weighty realities. It has shown us that God—Truth and Love in person—desired to suffer for us and with us. Bernard of Clairvaux coined the marvelous expression: *Impassibilis est Deus, sed non incompassibilis*[29]—God cannot suffer, but he can *suffer with*. Man is worth so much to God that he himself became man in order to *suffer with* man in an utterly real way—in flesh and blood—as is revealed to us in the account of Jesus' Passion. Hence in all human suffering we are joined by one who experiences and carries that suffering *with* us; hence *con-solatio* is present in all suffering, the consolation of God's compassionate love—and so the star of hope rises. Certainly, in our many different sufferings and trials we always need the lesser and greater hopes too—a kind visit, the healing of internal and external wounds, a favorable resolution of a crisis, and so on. In our lesser trials these kinds of hope may even be sufficient. But in truly great trials, where I must make a definitive decision to place the truth before my own welfare, career and possessions, I need the certitude of that true, great hope of which we have spoken here. For this too we need witnesses—martyrs—who have given themselves totally, so as to show us the way—day after day. We need them if we are to prefer goodness to comfort, even in the little choices we face each day—knowing that this is how we live life to the full. Let us say it once again: the capacity to suffer for the sake of the truth is the measure of humanity. Yet this capacity to suffer depends on the type and extent of the hope that we bear within us and build upon. The saints were able to make the great journey of human existence in the way that Christ had done before them, because they were brimming with great hope.

40. I would like to add here another brief comment with some relevance for everyday living. There used to be a form of devotion—perhaps less practiced today but quite widespread not long ago—that

included the idea of "offering up" the minor daily hardships that continually strike at us like irritating "jabs," thereby giving them a meaning. Of course, there were some exaggerations and perhaps unhealthy applications of this devotion, but we need to ask ourselves whether there may not after all have been something essential and helpful contained within it. What does it mean to offer something up? Those who did so were convinced that they could insert these little annoyances into Christ's great "com-passion" so that they somehow became part of the treasury of compassion so greatly needed by the human race. In this way, even the small inconveniences of daily life could acquire meaning and contribute to the economy of good and of human love. Maybe we should consider whether it might be judicious to revive this practice ourselves.

III. Judgment as a setting for learning and practicing hope

41. At the conclusion of the central section of the Church's great *Credo*—the part that recounts the mystery of Christ, from his eternal birth of the Father and his temporal birth of the Virgin Mary, through his Cross and Resurrection to the second coming—we find the phrase: "he will come again in glory to judge the living and the dead." From the earliest times, the prospect of the Judgment has influenced Christians in their daily living as a criterion by which to order their present life, as a summons to their conscience, and at the same time as hope in God's justice. Faith in Christ has never looked merely backwards or merely upwards, but always also forwards to the hour of justice that the Lord repeatedly proclaimed. This looking ahead has given Christianity its importance for the present moment. In the arrangement of Christian sacred buildings, which were intended to make visible the historic and cosmic breadth of faith in Christ, it became customary to depict the

Lord returning as a king—the symbol of hope—at the east end; while the west wall normally portrayed the Last Judgment as a symbol of our responsibility for our lives—a scene which followed and accompanied the faithful as they went out to resume their daily routine. As the iconography of the Last Judgment developed, however, more and more prominence was given to its ominous and frightening aspects, which obviously held more fascination for artists than the splendor of hope, often all too well concealed beneath the horrors.

42. In the modern era, the idea of the Last Judgment has faded into the background: Christian faith has been individualized and primarily oriented towards the salvation of the believer's own soul, while reflection on world history is largely dominated by the idea of progress. The fundamental content of awaiting a final Judgment, however, has not disappeared: it has simply taken on a totally different form. The atheism of the nineteenth and twentieth centuries is—in its origins and aims—a type of moralism: a protest against the injustices of the world and of world history. A world marked by so much injustice, innocent suffering, and cynicism of power cannot be the work of a good God. A God with responsibility for such a world would not be a just God, much less a good God. It is for the sake of morality that this God has to be contested. Since there is no God to create justice, it seems man himself is now called to establish justice. If in the face of this world's suffering, protest against God is understandable, the claim that humanity can and must do what no God actually does or is able to do is both presumptuous and intrinsically false. It is no accident that this idea has led to the greatest forms of cruelty and violations of justice; rather, it is grounded in the intrinsic falsity of the claim. A world which has to create its own justice is a world without hope. No one and nothing can answer for centuries of suffering.

No one and nothing can guarantee that the cynicism of power—whatever beguiling ideological mask it adopts—will cease to dominate the world. This is why the great thinkers of the Frankfurt School, Max Horkheimer and Theodor W. Adorno, were equally critical of atheism and theism. Horkheimer radically excluded the possibility of ever finding a this-worldly substitute for God, while at the same time he rejected the image of a good and just God. In an extreme radicalization of the Old Testament prohibition of images, he speaks of a "longing for the totally Other" that remains inaccessible—a cry of yearning directed at world history. Adorno also firmly upheld this total rejection of images, which naturally meant the exclusion of any "image" of a loving God. On the other hand, he also constantly emphasized this "negative" dialectic and asserted that justice—true justice—would require a world "where not only present suffering would be wiped out, but also that which is irrevocably past would be undone."[30] This, would mean, however—to express it with positive and hence, for him, inadequate symbols—that there can be no justice without a resurrection of the dead. Yet this would have to involve "the resurrection of the flesh, something that is totally foreign to idealism and the realm of Absolute spirit."[31]

43. Christians likewise can and must constantly learn from the strict rejection of images that is contained in God's first commandment (cf. *Ex* 20:4). The truth of negative theology was highlighted by the Fourth Lateran Council, which explicitly stated that however great the similarity that may be established between Creator and creature, the dissimilarity between them is always greater.[32] In any case, for the believer the rejection of images cannot be carried so far that one ends up, as Horkheimer and Adorno would like, by saying "no" to both theses—theism and atheism. God has given himself an "image": in Christ who was made man. In him

who was crucified, the denial of false images of God is taken to an extreme. God now reveals his true face in the figure of the sufferer who shares man's God-forsaken condition by taking it upon himself. This innocent sufferer has attained the certitude of hope: there is a God, and God can create justice in a way that we cannot conceive, yet we can begin to grasp it through faith. Yes, there is a resurrection of the flesh.[33] There is justice.[34] There is an "undoing" of past suffering, a reparation that sets things aright. For this reason, faith in the Last Judgment is first and foremost hope—the need for which was made abundantly clear in the upheavals of recent centuries. I am convinced that the question of justice constitutes the essential argument, or in any case the strongest argument, in favor of faith in eternal life. The purely individual need for a fulfillment that is denied to us in this life, for an everlasting love that we await, is certainly an important motive for believing that man was made for eternity; but only in connection with the impossibility that the injustice of history should be the final word does the necessity for Christ's return and for new life become fully convincing.

44. To protest against God in the name of justice is not helpful. A world without God is a world without hope (cf. *Eph* 2:12). Only God can create justice. And faith gives us the certainty that he does so. The image of the Last Judgment is not primarily an image of terror, but an image of hope; for us it may even be the decisive image of hope. Is it not also a frightening image? I would say: it is an image that evokes responsibility, an image, therefore, of that fear of which Saint Hilary spoke when he said that all our fear has its place in love.[35] God is justice and creates justice. This is our consolation and our hope. And in his justice there is also grace. This we know by turning our gaze to the crucified and risen Christ. Both these things—justice and grace—must be seen in their

correct inner relationship. Grace does not cancel out justice. It does not make wrong into right. It is not a sponge which wipes everything away, so that whatever someone has done on earth ends up being of equal value. Dostoevsky, for example, was right to protest against this kind of Heaven and this kind of grace in his novel *The Brothers Karamazov*. Evildoers, in the end, do not sit at table at the eternal banquet beside their victims without distinction, as though nothing had happened. Here I would like to quote a passage from Plato which expresses a premonition of just judgment that in many respects remains true and salutary for Christians too. Albeit using mythological images, he expresses the truth with an unambiguous clarity, saying that in the end souls will stand naked before the judge. It no longer matters what they once were in history, but only what they are in truth: "Often, when it is the king or some other monarch or potentate that he (the judge) has to deal with, he finds that there is no soundness in the soul whatever; he finds it scourged and scarred by the various acts of perjury and wrong-doing . . . ; it is twisted and warped by lies and vanity, and nothing is straight because truth has had no part in its development. Power, luxury, pride, and debauchery have left it so full of disproportion and ugliness that when he has inspected it (he) sends it straight to prison, where on its arrival it will undergo the appropriate punishment . . . Sometimes, though, the eye of the judge lights on a different soul which has lived in purity and truth . . . then he is struck with admiration and sends him to the isles of the blessed."[36] In the parable of the rich man and Lazarus (cf. *Lk* 16:19-31), Jesus admonishes us through the image of a soul destroyed by arrogance and opulence, who has created an impassable chasm between himself and the poor man; the chasm of being trapped within material pleasures; the chasm of forgetting the other, of incapacity to love, which then becomes a burning and unquenchable thirst. We must note that in this parable Jesus is not referring to the final destiny after the Last Judgment, but is taking up a notion found, *inter alia*, in early Judaism, namely that of an intermediate state between death and resurrection, a state in which the final sentence is yet to be pronounced.

45. This early Jewish idea of an intermediate state includes the view that these souls are not simply in a sort of temporary custody but, as the parable of the rich man illustrates, are already being punished or are experiencing a provisional form of bliss. There is also the idea that this state can involve purification and heal-ing which mature the soul for communion with God. The early Church took up these concepts, and in the Western Church they gradually developed into the doctrine of Purgatory. We do not need to examine here the complex historical paths of this develop-ment; it is enough to ask what it actually means. With death, our life-choice becomes definitive—our life stands before the judge. Our choice, which in the course of an entire life takes on a certain shape, can have a variety of forms. There can be people who have totally destroyed their desire for truth and readiness to love, peo-ple for whom everything has become a lie, people who have lived for hatred and have suppressed all love within themselves. This is a terrifying thought, but alarming profiles of this type can be seen in certain figures of our own history. In such people all would be beyond remedy and the destruction of good would be irrevocable: this is what we mean by the word *Hell*.[37] On the other hand there can be people who are utterly pure, completely permeated by God, and thus fully open to their neighbors—people for whom commu-nion with God even now gives direction to their entire being and whose journey towards God only brings to fulfillment what they already are.[38]

46. Yet we know from experience that neither case is normal in human life. For the great majority of people—we may suppose—there remains in the depths of their being an ultimate interior

49

openness to truth, to love, to God. In the concrete choices of life, however, it is covered over by ever new compromises with evil—much filth covers purity, but the thirst for purity remains and it still constantly re-emerges from all that is base and remains present in the soul. What happens to such individuals when they appear before the Judge? Will all the impurity they have amassed through life suddenly cease to matter? What else might occur? Saint Paul, in his *First Letter to the Corinthians*, gives us an idea of the differing impact of God's judgment according to each person's particular circumstances. He does this using images which in some way try to express the invisible, without it being possible for us to conceptualize these images—simply because we can neither see into the world beyond death nor do we have any experience of it. Paul begins by saying that Christian life is built upon a common foundation: Jesus Christ. This foundation endures. If we have stood firm on this foundation and built our life upon it, we know that it cannot be taken away from us even in death. Then Paul continues: "Now if any one builds on the foundation with gold, silver, precious stones, wood, hay, straw—each man's work will become manifest; for the Day will disclose it, because it will be revealed with fire, and the fire will test what sort of work each one has done. If the work which any man has built on the foundation survives, he will receive a reward. If any man's work is burned up, he will suffer loss, though he himself will be saved, but only as through fire" (*1 Cor* 3:12-15). In this text, it is in any case evident that our salvation can take different forms, that some of what is built may be burned down, that in order to be saved we personally have to pass through "fire" so as to become fully open to receiving God and able to take our place at the table of the eternal marriage-feast.

47. Some recent theologians are of the opinion that the fire which both burns and saves is Christ himself, the Judge and Savior. The

encounter with him is the decisive act of judgment. Before his gaze all falsehood melts away. This encounter with him, as it burns us, transforms and frees us, allowing us to become truly ourselves. All that we build during our lives can prove to be mere straw, pure bluster, and it collapses. Yet in the pain of this encounter, when the impurity and sickness of our lives become evident to us, there lies salvation. His gaze, the touch of his heart heals us through an undeniably painful transformation "as through fire." But it is a blessed pain, in which the holy power of his love sears through us like a flame, enabling us to become totally ourselves and thus totally of God. In this way the interrelation between justice and grace also becomes clear: the way we live our lives is not immaterial, but our defilement does not stain us forever if we have at least continued to reach out towards Christ, towards truth and towards love. Indeed, it has already been burned away through Christ's Passion. At the moment of judgment we experience and we absorb the overwhelming power of his love over all the evil in the world and in ourselves. The pain of love becomes our salvation and our joy. It is clear that we cannot calculate the "duration" of this transforming burning in terms of the chronological measurements of this world. The transforming "moment" of this encounter eludes earthly time-reckoning—it is the heart's time, it is the time of "passage" to communion with God in the Body of Christ.[39] The judgment of God is hope, both because it is justice and because it is grace. If it were merely grace, making all earthly things cease to matter, God would still owe us an answer to the question about justice—the crucial question that we ask of history and of God. If it were merely justice, in the end it could bring only fear to us all. The incarnation of God in Christ has so closely linked the two together—judgment and grace—that justice is firmly established: we all work out our salvation "with fear and trembling" (*Phil* 2:12). Nevertheless grace allows us all to hope, and to go trustfully to meet the Judge whom we know as our "advocate," or *parakletos* (cf. *1 Jn* 2:1).

48. A further point must be mentioned here, because it is important for the practice of Christian hope. Early Jewish thought includes the idea that one can help the deceased in their intermediate state through prayer (see for example *2 Macc* 12:38-45; first century BC). The equivalent practice was readily adopted by Christians and is common to the Eastern and Western Church. The East does not recognize the purifying and expiatory suffering of souls in the afterlife, but it does acknowledge various levels of beatitude and of suffering in the intermediate state. The souls of the departed can, however, receive "solace and refreshment" through the Eucharist, prayer and almsgiving. The belief that love can reach into the afterlife, that reciprocal giving and receiving is possible, in which our affection for one another continues beyond the limits of death—this has been a fundamental conviction of Christianity throughout the ages and it remains a source of comfort today. Who would not feel the need to convey to their departed loved ones a sign of kindness, a gesture of gratitude or even a request for pardon? Now a further question arises: if "Purgatory" is simply purification through fire in the encounter with the Lord, Judge and Savior, how can a third person intervene, even if he or she is particularly close to the other? When we ask such a question, we should recall that no man is an island, entire of itself. Our lives are involved with one another, through innumerable interactions they are linked together. No one lives alone. No one sins alone. No one is saved alone. The lives of others continually spill over into mine: in what I think, say, do and achieve. And conversely, my life spills over into that of others: for better and for worse. So my prayer for another is not something extraneous to that person, something external, not even after death. In the interconnectedness of Being, my gratitude to the other—my prayer for him—can play a small part in his purification. And for that there is no need to convert earthly time into God's time: in the communion of souls simple

52

terrestrial time is superseded. It is never too late to touch the heart of another, nor is it ever in vain. In this way we further clarify an important element of the Christian concept of hope. Our hope is always essentially also hope for others; only thus is it truly hope for me too.[40] As Christians we should never limit ourselves to asking: how can I save myself? We should also ask: what can I do in order that others may be saved and that for them too the star of hope may rise? Then I will have done my utmost for my own personal salvation as well.

Mary, Star of Hope

49. With a hymn composed in the eighth or ninth century, thus for over a thousand years, the Church has greeted Mary, the Mother of God, as "Star of the Sea": *Ave maris stella*. Human life is a journey. Towards what destination? How do we find the way? Life is like a voyage on the sea of history, often dark and stormy, a voyage in which we watch for the stars that indicate the route. The true stars of our life are the people who have lived good lives. They are lights of hope. Certainly, Jesus Christ is the true light, the sun that has risen above all the shadows of history. But to reach him we also need lights close by—people who shine with his light and so guide us along our way. Who more than Mary could be a star of hope for us? With her "yes" she opened the door of our world to God himself; she became the living Ark of the Covenant, in whom God took flesh, became one of us, and pitched his tent among us (cf. *Jn* 1:14).

50. So we cry to her: Holy Mary, you belonged to the humble and great souls of Israel who, like Simeon, were "looking for the consolation of Israel" (*Lk* 2:25) and hoping, like Anna, "for the redemption of Jerusalem" (*Lk* 2:38). Your life was thoroughly imbued with the sacred scriptures of Israel which spoke of hope, of the promise made to Abraham and his descendants (cf. *Lk* 1:55). In this way we can appreciate the holy fear that overcame you when the angel of the Lord appeared to you and told you that you would give birth to the One who was the hope of Israel, the One awaited by the world. Through you, through your "yes," the hope of the ages became reality, entering this world and its history. You bowed low before the greatness of this task and gave your consent: "Behold, I am the handmaid of the Lord; let it be to me according to your word" (*Lk* 1:38). When you hastened with holy joy across the mountains of Judea to see your cousin Elizabeth, you became the

image of the Church to come, which carries the hope of the world in her womb across the mountains of history. But alongside the joy which, with your *Magnificat,* you proclaimed in word and song for all the centuries to hear, you also knew the dark sayings of the prophets about the suffering of the servant of God in this world. Shining over his birth in the stable at Bethlehem, there were angels in splendor who brought the good news to the shepherds, but at the same time the lowliness of God in this world was all too palpable. The old man Simeon spoke to you of the sword which would pierce your soul (cf. *Lk* 2:35), of the sign of contradiction that your Son would be in this world. Then, when Jesus began his public ministry, you had to step aside, so that a new family could grow, the family which it was his mission to establish and which would be made up of those who heard his word and kept it (cf. *Lk* 11:27f.). Notwithstanding the great joy that marked the beginning of Jesus' ministry, in the synagogue of Nazareth you must already have experienced the truth of the saying about the "sign of contradiction" (cf. *Lk* 4:28ff.). In this way you saw the growing power of hostility and rejection which built up around Jesus until the hour of the Cross, when you had to look upon the Savior of the world, the heir of David, the Son of God dying like a failure, exposed to mockery, between criminals. Then you received the word of Jesus: "Woman, behold, your Son!" (*Jn* 19:26). From the Cross you received a new mission. From the Cross you became a mother in a new way: the mother of all those who believe in your Son Jesus and wish to follow him. The sword of sorrow pierced your heart. Did hope die? Did the world remain definitively without light, and life without purpose? At that moment, deep down, you probably listened again to the word spoken by the angel in answer to your fear at the time of the Annunciation: "Do not be afraid, Mary!" (*Lk* 1:30). How many times had the Lord, your Son, said the same thing to his disciples: do not be afraid! In your heart, you heard this word again during the night of Golgotha. Before the hour of his betrayal he had said to his disciples: "Be of good cheer, I have overcome the world" (*Jn* 16:33). "Let not your hearts be troubled, neither let them be afraid" (*Jn* 14:27). "Do not be afraid, Mary!" In that hour at Nazareth the angel had also said to you: "Of his kingdom there will be no end" (*Lk* 1:33). Could it have ended before it began? No, at the foot of the Cross, on the strength of Jesus' own word, you became the mother of believers.

In this faith, which even in the darkness of Holy Saturday bore the certitude of hope, you made your way towards Easter morning. The joy of the Resurrection touched your heart and united you in a new way to the disciples, destined to become the family of Jesus through faith. In this way you were in the midst of the community of believers, who in the days following the Ascension prayed with one voice for the gift of the Holy Spirit (cf. *Acts* 1:14) and then received that gift on the day of Pentecost. The "Kingdom" of Jesus was not as might have been imagined. It began in that hour, and of this "Kingdom" there will be no end. Thus you remain in the midst of the disciples as their Mother, as the Mother of hope. Holy Mary, Mother of God, our Mother, teach us to believe, to hope, to love with you. Show us the way to his Kingdom! Star of the Sea, shine upon us and guide us on our way!

Given in Rome, at Saint Peter's, on 30 November, the Feast of Saint Andrew the Apostle, in the year 2007, the third of my Pontificate.

NOTES

1   *Corpus Inscriptionum Latinarum* VI, no. 26003.

2   Cf. *Dogmatic Poems,* V, 53-64: PG 37, 428-429.

3   Cf. *Catechism of the Catholic Church,* 1817-1821.

4   *Summa Theologiae,* II-IIae, q. 4, a. 1.

5   H. Köster in *Theological Dictionary of the New Testament* VIII (1972), p. 586.

6   *De excessu fratris sui Satyri,* II, 47: CSEL 73, 274.

7   *Ibid.,* II, 46: CSEL 73, 273.

8   Cf. Ep. 130 *Ad Probam* 14, 25-15, 28: CSEL 44, 68-73.

9   Cf. *Catechism of the Catholic Church,* 1025.

10   Jean Giono, *Les vraies richesses* (1936), Preface, Paris 1992, pp. 18-20; quoted in Henri de Lubac, *Catholicisme. Aspects sociaux du dogme,* Paris 1983, p. VII.

11   Ep. 130 *Ad Probam* 13, 24: CSEL 44, 67.

12   *Sententiae* III, 118: CCL 6/2, 215.

13   Cf. *ibid.,* III, 71: CCL 6/2, 107-108.

14   *Novum Organum* I, 117.

15   Cf. *ibid.,* I, 129.

16   Cf. *New Atlantis.*

17   In *Werke* IV, ed. W. Weischedel (1956), p. 777.

18   I. Kant, *Das Ende aller Dinge,* in *Werke* VI, ed. W. Weischedel (1964), p. 190.

19   Chapters on charity, *Centuria* 1, ch. 1: PG 90, 965.

20   Cf. *ibid.:* PG 90, 962-966.

21   *Conf.* X 43, 70: CSEL 33, 279.

22   *Sermo* 340, 3: PL 38, 1484; cf. F. Van der Meer, *Augustine the Bishop,* London and New York 1961, p. 268.

23   *Sermo* 339, 4: PL 38, 1481.

24   *Conf.* X 43, 69: CSEL 33, 279.

25   Cf. *Catechism of the Catholic Church,* 2657.

26   Cf. *In 1 Ioannis* 4, 6: PL 35, 2008f.

27   *Testimony of Hope,* Boston 2000, pp. 121ff.

28   The Liturgy of the Hours, Office of Readings, 24 November.

29   *Sermones in Cant., Sermo* 26, 5: PL 183, 906.

30   *Negative Dialektik* (1966), Third part, III, 11, in *Gesammelte Schriften* VI, Frankfurt am Main 1973, p. 395.

31   *Ibid.*, Second part, p. 207.

32   DS 806.

33   Cf. *Catechism of the Catholic Church*, 988-1004.

34   Cf. *ibid.*, 1040.

35   Cf. *Tractatus super Psalmos, Ps* 127, 1-3: CSEL 22, 628-630.

36   *Gorgias* 525a-526c.

37   Cf. *Catechism of the Catholic Church*, 1033-1037.

38   Cf. *ibid.*, 1023-1029.

39   Cf. *Catechism of the Catholic Church*, 1030-1032.

40   Cf. *Catechism of the Catholic Church*, 1032.